Ways into Science

Light and Dark

Written by Peter Riley

W
FRANKLIN WATTS
LONDON·SYDNEY

This edition 2008

Franklin Watts
338 Euston Road, London NW1 3BH

Franklin Watts Australia
Level 17/207 Kent Street
Sydney, NSW 2000

Series editor: Rachel Cooke
Assistant editor: Adrian Cole
Series design: Jason Anscomb
Design: Michael Leaman Design Partnership
Photography: Ray Moller (unless
otherwise credited)

A CIP catalogue record for this book
is available from the British Library

ISBN 978 0 7496 8330 6

Dewey Classification 535

Printed in Malaysia

Picture credits:
Image Bank/Harald Sund p. 13; Pictor International pp. 8,
9, 10, 11; The Stock Market/David Keaton p. 18

Franklin Watts is a division of Hachette Children's Books,
an Hachette Livre UK company.

Contents

Light

When it is light,
we can see.

We can see
where
things are.

We can see
their colours.

Dark

When there is no light, it is dark. We cannot see anything.

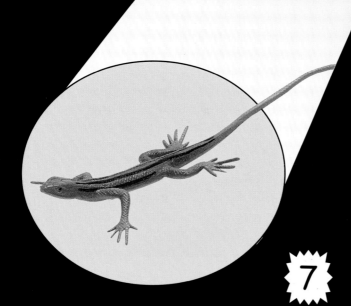

Switch on a light in the dark and you can see again.

The  Sun

The Sun gives out light.
It lets us see all around.

You must not look at the
Sun. It can burn your eyes.

Sometimes, clouds stop some
sunlight coming to us.
It becomes darker but
we can still see.
Is it sunny or cloudy today?

Night

At night the Sun is not in the sky. It is dark. But sometimes the Moon and stars can be seen in the night sky.

The Moon shines with a steady light. The stars twinkle.

Look for the Moon and stars tonight. Can you see them?

Other things light up the dark
during the night, too.

What things in this picture
are lighting up the dark?
How do you light up
the dark at home?

Light makers

An electric lamp makes light.
It can light up a whole room.

 A candle gives out a small amount of light.

Outside, a bonfire gives out lots of light.

What other things give out light?

Eye-spy

Aisha has made a box with a lid and a spy-hole. She puts a toy in the box.

Trevor looks through the spy-hole. He sees the toy.

Aisha puts on the lid.
Trevor looks through
the spy-hole again.

What do you think he
can see this time?
Turn the page to find out.

See the light

Trevor cannot see anything.
It is dark in the box.

Here is another test for you to try.

1. Put a toy in a box with a spy-hole in it.

2. Put tissue paper over the top of the box to hide the toy.

3. Cut one end off the lid and cover the box with this or some card.

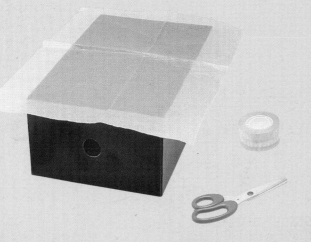

4. Ask a friend to look through the spy-hole. At first, your friend should not be able to see anything.

5. Now slowly slide the lid or card off the top.

Ask your friend to describe what he or she sees. How does it change as the card moves and more light gets into the box?

17

Shadows

Sometimes, things block out light and make shadows.

The Sun is shining behind this tree. The tree blocks out the light. It makes a dark shadow in front of it.

If you stand in a tree's shadow, you are in the shade.

Paul shines his
torch on a toy.

Aisha measures
the shadow.

Paul shines his torch from higher up.
What happens to the shadow?
Find out on the next page.

Long and short

If the torch is higher up, the toy's shadow gets shorter.

When Paul puts the torch down again the shadow gets longer.

Look at your shadow outside on a sunny day. Your shadow changes during the day. In the morning, when the Sun is low, it is long.

At lunch time, when the Sun is high in the sky, your shadow is short. Ask someone to measure it each time.

Will it be long or short at the end of the day?

21

Moving shadows

These are shadow puppets. They make shadows.

When the puppet moves, the shadow moves too.

How can you make your shadow move?

Put a piece
of paper
under a lamp.

Hold a pen near the paper.
The pen makes a sharp,
dark shadow on the paper.

Slowly lift the pen
up, away from the
paper. What
happens to
the pen's
shadow?

It's  shiny

Some things are shiny.

They shine because they are very smooth. When light strikes them it is reflected in strong beams.

This shoe is polished smooth. Light reflects strongly off it.

This mirror reflects beams of light.

Things that are not very smooth do not shine much.

When light reflects off them, it is broken up and does not make strong beams. The things look dull.

These stripy socks do not shine.

The paints do not shine even though they are brightly coloured.

Sort them out

Sort these objects into two groups: shiny things and dull things.

woolly hat

paints

teaspoon

bottle

tin can

hand mirror

wooden brick

26

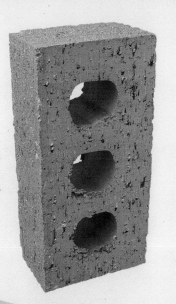

clay
brick

sponge

cardboard

orange

Someone has already started sorting and put their results on a pictogram. Copy this pictogram and finish it off.

Shiny	Dull
bottle	paints

What other objects can you add to each group?

27

Useful words

beam - a ray of light.

dull - when an object does not shine because its surface is not smooth.

mirror - a sheet of glass with a shiny metal coating on the back that reflects light.

Moon - the ball of rock that moves around the Earth. The Moon does not give out light. We only see it when the Sun's light reflects off it.

reflects - the way light hits and bounces off objects.

shade - when you are in a shadow and out of the sunlight.

shadow - the dark area that is made when an object, like a tree, blocks out light.

shiny - when an object reflects strong beams of light.

stars - objects in space which give out light.

Sun - the nearest star to Earth which provides most of our light.

Some  answers

Here are some answers to the questions we have asked in this book. Don't worry if you had some different answers to ours; you may be right, too. Talk through your answers with other people and see if you can explain why they are right.

page 9
This depends whether it is a rainy or a sunny day. If there are clouds in the sky, what do they look like? Try using words like thin and thick, fluffy and hazy to describe what you see.

page 10
It is best to look into the night sky away from other bright lights, but don't go out on your own. If the sky is clear of cloud you should see the Moon and stars.

page 11
Car headlamps, street lamps and shop signs all light up the dark. At home you probably use electric lamps to light up the dark.

page 13
Television screens, camera flashes, stars, the Sun but not the Moon (see page 28) all give out light.

page 17
At first your friend will not be able to see anything. Slowly, as more light hits the toy, your friend will see its shape and colour become clearer and brighter.

page 21
At the end of the day the shadow will be longer because the Sun is lower in the sky (see page 20).

page 22
You can change any shadow by moving the object that casts it. Try moving your hands to make different shapes.

page 23
As the picture shows, the pen's shadow gets fuzzier and larger as the pen moves away from the paper, towards the light.

page 27
This answer depends on what objects you find to add to your collection. Every object can be shiny or dull, or sometimes both, such as a shiny spoon that has a dull wooden handle. Shiny objects include: the cover of this book, cooking foil, a metal paperclip; dull objects include: a potato crisp, a football, a woolly jumper.

Index

About this book

Ways into Science is designed to encourage children to begin to think about their everyday world in a scientific way, examining cause and effect through close observation, recording their results and discussing what they have seen. Here are some pointers to gain the maximum use from **Light and Dark**.

• Working through this book will introduce the basic concepts of light and also some of the language structures and vocabulary associated with it (for example, comparatives such as shiny and dull). This will prepare the child for more formal work later in the school curriculum.

• On pages 15 and 19 children are invited to predict the results of a particular action. Ensure you discuss the reason for any answer they give in some depth before turning over the page. In both these cases there is only one accurate answer, but don't worry if they get it wrong. Discuss the reasons for the answer they gave then create other scenarios and get the children to predict the results again.

• Use pages 6 and 14-17 to introduce the idea of different strengths of light. For example, in dim light we can see shapes of things, but not always their colour.

• Page 13 could be used to make the child aware that most objects do not give out light. We see them by the light they reflect, which is addressed on pages 24-27. You could use the information provided as a base for further study. For example, discuss how the Moon acts like a very large mirror, reflecting sunlight, even when the Sun is not in the sky.

• On pages 26-27, explore the relationship between shiny and dull objects. Do shiny objects always have a smooth surface? What about crumpled aluminium foil? Can an object be both shiny and dull? For example, if you breathe on a spoon it becomes dull.